Have Pity on My Guitar

MAHMOUD S KAWASH

Published by Aamir Abdullah, 2024.

While every precaution has been taken in the preparation of this book, the publisher assumes no responsibility for errors or omissions, or for damages resulting from the use of the information contained herein.

HAVE PITY ON MY GUITAR

First edition. September 25, 2024.

Copyright © 2024 MAHMOUD S KAWASH.

ISBN: 979-8227958853

Written by MAHMOUD S KAWASH.

Table of Contents

<u>Dedication</u>

This book is a dedication to

my family at home land and abroad.

I especially dedicate it to my parents,

(May Allah have mercy on them)

My wife, my children, my sisters,

my brothers, and my close friends.

HAVE PITY ON MY GUITAR

MAHMOUD S KAWASH

TITLE: Have Pity on My Guitar
POET: Mahmoud S Kawash (Denmark)
Designed, Edited and Proofread by:
Aamir Abdullah
Formatted by: Momina Aamir
Published in: September 2024
Edition: 1st
Author Contact: +45-27-54-1111
Discourse I Sol E-book Publishers (Pakistan)

PREFACE

PATRIOTISM AND ROMANICISM ARE IN THEIR VEINS
Review of the creativity of Mahmoud Said Kawash

T

here are no boundaries for literature "poetry and verse" in the world and every country has people, who devoted a great part of their lives to literature. In some aspects of life these people are like minded. Both Patriotism and Romanticism occupy a great part of their lives and love to their native land appears from their veins. One of these people is Mahmoud Said Kawash.

Mahmoud Said Kawash is a Palestinian - Danish poet for humanity, writer and researcher, who was born in Mirun - Safad, in the upper

Galilee of now occupied Palestine.

His life and creative line is very rich and colourful.

Mahmoud Said Kawash is highly educated and has succeeded in the area of literature "poetry and verse", culture, education and press.

Mahmoud Said Kawash covers different themes in his books. Reading his poems takes the reader through different stages of social and poetry life. However, the golden line of his creativity is his love for his nationality, people and motherland. His creative diversity makes him a golden pen holder.

As an international poet, he participated in many of the famous international anthologies such as "Inner Child Press International - W.A.R. We Are Revolution - Poets for Humanity - 2020", "Inner Child Press International & The Year of the Poet - Poetry, the best of 2020 - Poets of the world", "ATUNIS GALAXY ANTHOLOGIES 2021, 2022, 2025 WORLD POETRY", "The whispers of Soflay vol. 4 - Yearly Anthology of Poetry 2022", "Jara Foundation Nepal - Creative Bridge 2022 International Poetry Anthology", "WORLD CONTEMPORARY POETS, VOL.2". He is also a "Moderator" or a "Top Contributor" in many "International Literary Daily and weekly Magazines".

His success took Mahmoud Said Kawash to every country and every poetry lover's home. One of those poetry lovers is me, Ismayilova Mesma Aliyulla gizi.

"His distinguished activity interested me, so I translated one of his poems - The call of the great return - to Azerbaijani, and I hope that I can translate many more of his beautiful poems."

Respect and success from Azerbaijan

Ismayilova Mesma Aliyulla gizi

Azerbaijan

Doctor in philosophy and philology and a senior teacher - translator

Azerbaijan State Pedagogical University

HAVE PITY ON MY GUITAR

My heart drifted away
How can I forget
That night when love called me
Her shadow pierced within
Tangling with my blood
Standing at her door... Come, I whispered
Her bust longing for an embrace
She threw herself swiftly, unhesitant
In the arms of her fervent lover
I scented her ecstatic wet lips
That blasted pure nectar
Feeling her concealed eagerness
I stealthily touched her breast
Whose temperament so suave, so intense
My lips almost touching hers
Burning an ardent flame
I gathered my strengths to hold her tight
And felt her hasty bliss
Revealing her divine thick lips
Soon emerged redness on her cheeks
Reminding me of the moment

When the sun blends with the horizon
Oh virgin! In the depths of your fine ear
Live the murmurs that I solicit you to hear
I beseech you to pierce my broken heart
Brunette
Blonde
My days with you are scarce
Hoping you fulfil your promise
Pity my guitar! Break the serment
Oh virgin
For this ardent fiery passion
Slowly! I plead
My torment, my persecutor
For my blood is effusively flowing
Brunette
Blonde
Be compassionate
Appease my shattered feelings
Am I not your revered sacrilege
Her promised affection lurked around me
Intoxicated by her breath
I remove her veil to sense her
Feeling her every supple curve
My insatiable desire is quenched at last.
I never forget that night
When love called me and my heart drifted away
I never forget how her shadow pierced within
Tangling with my blood.

Note (1):
The word "serment" means "a solemn promise, usually invoking a divine witness, regarding the future acts or behaviour".
It is a French word in origin and its translation in English:
nom masculin
1 (devant une autorité)
oath
déclarer sous serment
to declare on (anglais britannique)
ou under oath
prêter serment
to take the oath
un serment professionnel
a professional oath.
Note (2): This poem was published in (Whisper of Soflay – volume 4 – yearly anthology – 2022 – pages 362, 363 and 364)

Whispers of Soflay Vol 4
Yearly Anthology of Poetry
Rehmat Changaizi
Alicia Minjarez

A LETTER FROM THE EXILE

"Three parts"

Part 1: <u>CRY OF A PALESTINIAN IN THE EXILE</u>

No No, I am not there
No, I am not there anymore
I was there, now I am here
Here, in a revolting world
Sad, gloomy, senseless
Merciless and unloving
In a world drenched with frets
Sorrows and boredom
Choked by dullness, ample of monotony
Aimless and hopeless
With no beginning and no end
Strident with cries, lament and pain
Drenched with grief
Now I am here in a world of cries
A strange world
Feeding from the earth, kissing the pebbles
Spending long nights, playing my chords
Contemplating the moon
And barely closing my eyes
The nights of my foreignness are long
Heavy, killing the daylight
Filled with gloom, aimless, cursed
Cursing every grain of earth

Cursing stones, trees and people.

Part 2: A LOVER'S BEAUTIFUL HYMN

Before now, I was there
Dwelling on the hills of my village
With my fellow men
Uphill where the earth
Held my glory, breath and splendour
I was in Mirun
Where lie my origins
My identity, my people
My place of prayer
Where my flock crawled
Before now, I was there
Hopeful and joyful
Singing gleefully
Not knowing grief
Or tears of pain
Or cries or wails
Before now, I was there
Ambitious and optimistic
My path was long
Embracing the echoes in the way
Embracing my very roots
With blissful yearns
There was no sound
But a lover's beautiful hymn.

Part 3: IN A FRAUD WORLD

Now I am here, not there anymore
I am here
Embracing my pillow
Sleeping mournfully
In a world not of my own
A vast and wide world
I wish it were smaller
I have no other choice
But to embrace my pillow
Lie in my bed
Eat the soil, kiss the stones
My mind and soul overwhelmed by shrieks
They lower in tone
And suddenly holler the voice of destiny
Now I am here, in the world of riches
The world of the oppressors
Where the music of shrilling drums pierces ears
Now I am here...here I am
Though I will never ever, not in a million years
Feed from the earth, nor kiss the stones
In this fraud world, strange and odd
That belittles the wise
Uses the learned and clever
And disheartens a lover.

THE CALL OF THE GREAT RETURN

Torture me,

I'm a giant, grimacing with the dawn
I'm a hurricane, smashing tyranny at its doorsteps
Oppression fears me and panic stutters
Anger flows and rumbles through my handcuffs
That's my land, where people suffer and complain
That's my water, which turns into poison and gall
The peaks of Mirun call out: awareness is smiling
I love you and yearn to liberate my homeland
I love you and I only love my freedom
Torture me,
I'm a revolutionist, I sing my revolution
Torture me,
Burn the structure of my old fathers
Turn their glories into funerals for young orphans
Fill the land with misery, moans and tents
Seek help from neighbours, who embraced humiliation and slept
Worship dollars however and whenever you desire
I refuse the ingenuine "peace" they offer me
As long as my rights are thrown on the shelves of the UN
The call of return sends loud echoes all around
I love you and I only love my freedom
Torture me,
I'm a revolutionist, I sing my revolution
Note: Mirun is a village in the Upper Galilee of Palestine.

BE THE WAY

YOU SHOULD BE

Be the way you should be!!

Be you, only you!!
Don't ponder or stare at grim faces
Beware of being left to the malevolent hearts
Or seeking wilted roses and flowers
Beware not to turn your face to the left side
So as not to be sad and depressed
And not to feel despair and despondency
Who knows, you may reach the limit of refraction
And feel hopelessness and collapse
Turn right to see beautiful,
welcoming and smiling faces
And meet bright, innocent and pure white hearts
He who holds 'The book' with his
right hand is satisfied with his life
He who holds it with his left hand
would have wished it were fatal
Try to taste every feeling you encounter
Sweet, bitter or even gall
Because you know that there are
various races in the world
And different colours and varieties
Sometimes weird and uncomfortable
Try and try

Try and don't hesitate
Try and don't regret
Try to realize the type and shape of this colour
Try to perceive the meaning and effect of that taste
Endure the pricking of thorns that
you may trample one day
Be patient and agonized
No matter how enlarged and magnified
Perhaps this is a scourge for you
from the 'Lord of the World'
Don't be disheartened
Never be desperate of the mercy of God, Almighty
Whenever God loves someone,
He examines his patience
He, only He, is thanked for affliction
Don't ever be sad or depressed
Some people have spent half of
their life in grief and despair
For too many reasons
Some logical, others illogical
Some objective, others not objective
Some justified, others unjustified
Due to the loss of a lover or a dear friend
The loss of a dream or an illusion
And now they are nothing
Nothing at all
They dwell in a bleak room
They are neither satisfied nor convinced of anything
Do we remember them,
Or mention their names in an occasion or without?
Do we know anything about them?
No, no, no!!

Did they benefit from all of that!?
Did they reap anything from being isolated?!
Certainly not, neither
And a thousand no
How beautiful is it to look like
the sun shining among people
Others seek light, warmth and tenderness from you
They remember you if you're absent and only mention you with
good
They enjoy your presence, the sweetness of your tongue and your
manners
They yearn for the warmth of your existence, tenderness and feel
reassured
How beautiful is to look like a flower
That people strive to be adorned by
To be perfumed by its scent
To enjoy hugging and embracing it
How beautiful is to look like an opened book
Readers seek your friendship,
sitting and talking with you
Scoop out your beautiful and useful words and letters
Get fruitful, valuable and
abundant lessons and expressions
Life is full of excavations, watch out and be careful not to fall into
the evil of one of them
It is full of traps, be careful not
to get caught in one of them
It is full of rocks, be careful not to
stumble with one of them
And don't forget to put them together
to make a ladder for success
You climb on it and ascend to glory and eternity

Be the way you should be
Be you, only you!!
Congratulations for yourself and to others!!
Be the way you should be!!
Be you, only you.

Note "1":

Using 'his' or 'their' in the following line of poetry (Whenever God loves someone, He examines 'his or their' patience) depends on whether the addressed is singular or plural.

Note "2": This poem was published in (Inner Child Press International Anthology – W.A.R – We Are Revolution – Poets For Humanity) pages 54 & 55.

Inner Child Press International
presents
W.A.R.
We Are Revolution
Poets for Humanity

EVE, THE GREAT

Eve is Great
How great she is

Yes she is great
And the secret of her greatness is in her motherhood
In her tenderness, kindness and femininity
And in everything she has and does
Eve amazes me
Yes, she amazes me
She amazes me by attending her enduring passion
She is the first to express her love and show sympathy
She is the first to smile and to shed tears
And often her smiles and tears mix together
She is the first to show tenderness
To experience her tenderness, try when you are sick
Or pretend to be sick
Try and get sick
Then you will see her fear for you
And feel when she wipes your head
with her warm hand
Her hand is always warm!!
If you get sick and your temperature becomes high
Ask Eve to put her hand on your forehead
You will feel it's warmer than your forehead!!
How can this be when your temperature is high?
It is an amazing secret

Eve's warmth does not emit from
her blood as is the case for us
Rather, it always rushes from the warmth of her present emotion!!
You see Eve asleep and her hand on her baby
How to do that while she is sleeping?
Doesn't she move her hand with feeling, as we do?
It seems that Eve does not sleep at all
Rather, her passion always remains awake
She is always alert and ready
You can put your head on her shoulder
whenever you like
Even if she is angry with you
Put your head on her shoulder
You find her hand wiping your head automatically
Wonderful!!
Why can't you do that?
Really, Eve is amazing
No wonder God "Almighty" made her deserve the best company
No wonder He made Paradise under her feet
Amazing is Eve
And great is she
And great is Adam when he reads her better!!
Greetings and appreciation to you, dear Eve
You are the mother, the sister, the wife and the daughter
The auntie and the aunt
The Sweetie and the girlfriend
It is you whom "Prophet of Mercy" said:
"Have pity on her"
The Holy Prophet is truthful
Greetings and appreciation to you Eve,
Everywhere and anytime
Every moment and with every whisper!!

May Allah bless you
You are really great
How great you are Eve!!

Note: This poem was published in (Inner Child Press International & The Year OF The Poet – Poetry "the best of 2020" – Poets Of The World) – From page 414 to page 416.

AN EXCEPTIONAL WOMAN

He has known her as a gentle breeze
with her delicacy and sweetness
And as a transient and romantic dream with her compassion and
magnificence
The rainbow hides when she appears
with her smiling face
The poets' and writers' talent and inspiration flow with the sparkle
of her look
Sorrow and misery turn into joy and happiness with the warmth of
her whisper.
Despair and despondency turn into hope and optimism when peo-
ple accompany her
That was how he knew her!!
He knew her as she did not know herself
And as no one else knew her
Yes, so he knew her!!
He knew her as he did not know anyone else
Perhaps, as he will not know a similar or alternative
Amongst all the women, in all places and times
That was how he knew her!!
He knew her because he lived with her

Just as the parents, sisters and brothers did not
Just as uncles and aunts did not
He knew her more than the most faithful and loyal relatives and
friends
Yes, so he knew her!!
He loved her with his mind and heart
With bold and blatant feelings
He accepted her with her simplicity, slips of her tongue and inno-
cent mistakes
Since she knew him, she did not suffer from repression or depriva-
tion
With him she felt reassurance, security and safety
Yes, so he loved her!!
She did not know the meaning of life
as she did with him
And did not taste contentment and
love as she did with him
She said goodbye to innocence while
she was in his arms
She did that when Allah gave her
the permission to do so
That was how he knew her!!
She loved him with her instinct,
her chastity, and her spontaneity
With her weakness and strength
She loved him according to
her method, nature and temper
She loved him according to the
firm wisdom and strict traditions
She loved him in a gentle,
sweet, dreamy and romantic way
That was how she loved him!!

She was a half-sane, realistic, and
a wandering half-fictional
Half wise, quiet, crazy and revolting
Half civilized and half bedouin
Half submissive maid and half modern princess
Half innocent child and half genius woman
That's who she was!!
She was known by her love to literature,
culture, knowledge and science
She was known by her good
speech, social and public relation
She made him swing between
this world and the "hereafter"
Between the glow of the mind and
the rebellious passion
Between the super consciousness and
the extreme madness
That's how she was known!!
She knew how to forgive all his mistakes and slips
And calm all his nervousness and tension
And reduce his impulsion and recklessness
She knew how to make him an extraordinary and distinguished
husband
She transformed him from a rebellious man to a spontaneous ro-
mantic poet.
She transformed him from an arrogant
man to a sane and submissive child
It was not difficult for her to
make him diplomatic and flexible
Because she was honest and capable, in a time where feelings
turned into goods for sale and purchase

This is how she knew him and thus turned him into AN EXCEP-
TIONAL MAN!!
Yes!! Because she is AN EXCEPTIONAL WOMAN!!
She is truly AN EXCEPTIONAL WOMAN!!
Really, she is a woman!!
What a woman!!

*Note: This poem was published in (ATUNIS GALAXY ANTHOL-
OGY 2021) – From page 279 to 281.*
*ANTHOLOGY OF CONTEMPORARY WORLD POETRY –
ATUNIS POETRY*

ATUNIS GALAXY
ANTHOLOGY 2021
Demer Press

NEVER BE NEGATIVE

As love is not just how to find the right person
But how to create a right relationship
It's not how much love you have at the beginning
But how will the end of this love be
Marriage is so too!!
As wisdom is sometimes taken
from the mouth of the insane
Too many lessons are best learned
through pain and suffering
Sometimes, our visions clear only
after our eyes are washed with tears
Sometimes, we have to be broken,
so we can be whole again!!
Let the matter be understandable and clear to you:
If Allah, the Almighty made
the day to be completely perfect,
He wouldn't let you dream of
tomorrow and after tomorrow,
He wouldn't make them full
of pleasant and sad surprises,
He wouldn't give us the ability
to forget and overcome pain!!
Keep Positive, hopeful and optimist

Make people happy with your welcome smile
No charge for it, but it can change someone's life
Don't ever start your day
with broken pieces of yesterday
Every morning we wake up is
the first day of the rest of life
It is right that we can not help everyone,
But it is right too that everyone can help someone
Start your day with blessing someone
Never be negative, hopeless and pessimist
Allah, the Almighty, is the greatest
Whenever you feel like giving up,
Thinking of all the people would love to see you fail,
Never give up even till your last breath!!
If you want to be extremely happy in life
find someone who'll never get tired of kissing you
who'll hug you when you become jealous
who'll understandingly keep silent when you get mad
who'll squeeze your hand
when you're not in the mood
who'll plan and imagine your future with you
This is how you stay positive and never be negative!!
*<u>Note: This poem was published in (Whisper of Soflay – volume 4 –
yearly anthology – 2022 – pages 362, 363 and 364)</u>*

Whispers of Soflay Vol 4
Yearly Anthology of Poetry
Rehmat Changaizi
Alicia Minjarez

International Poetry Platform

Skylark Poetry Society

CERTIFICATE OF ACHIEVEMENT

PROUDLY PRESENTED TO

Mahmud S Kawash

Poem: Never Be Negative

WEEKLY POETRY CONTEST

THEME: POETRY FOR PEACE

Abu Forhad

Founder/ Director

SPS Team

02.04.22

SWEETHEART DIANA

Diana,
O innocence of days and happy dreaming
O fancy shore and glory of the blessed azure beaches
Oh nap of love and whisper of
longing in an abyssal canyon
Diana,
My guitar, lyre, and lute are within your hands
And in my lips the supplication is completed
So that you may decide to return as soon as you can
And in the heart you have a prayer for your existence
Diana,
This rose is from you, and
you are a descendant of roses
There is no perfume other than
the perfume of your cheeks
Oh heart's desire on the "settler" of heart and mind
Diana,
You who were my patience,
and the echo of my presence
Do you remember the glorious rituals of the oath
Or you already forgot the love poems I wrote for you?
Diana,
Oh sweetheart and the grace of my eye
Pity on my heart and come back

Oh honey of life come back, come as soon as you can Diana,
Hurry, come back and be generous and kind!!

DO NOT EVER BE A SERVILE SURRENDERER

Realizing that I was
about to leave

She fervently and warmly asked me to stay longer
I said to her: I would like to stay forever sweetheart
Because no matter how long our meeting is
It will not be enough to express the love I have for you
But I'm afraid of "envious eyes" which
might catch us together
I fear for you, lovely resident of my heart
This fear has no equal among lovers
I fear for you from the cold weather in the evening
I fear for you from the birds' loud peeping
I fear the pigeons and their murmuring in the sky
And their cooing if it increases and bothers you
I am even afraid of an envious angel
Jealous of your slender body when it tilts and bows
I am more affectionate to you than the dewdrop
And more affectionate than the breeze at dusk time
Impossibility among beloved ones is permissible
Do not assume that I am saying something impossible
But listen my angel once, just once
Do not surrender to love as a servile surrenderer
Do not ever be a servile surrenderer
Honey tastes sweet even when it is little
Longing no matter how much needs little sweet

See you, my soul, tomorrow or after
Seeking neighborhood and beautiful friendliness

NEIGHBOURHOOD DOE

Oh neighbourhood doe,
whose pastures are in my sides,
Will you take care of my heart
which deeply loves you,
Becomes so sad and burns by the fire of longing,
Does not like any amongst the
multitudes of beauties except you
Oh neighbourhood doe, my life dream,
My heart remains anxious about you
Despite the delights, I remain wailing in tears
I anxiously spend my nights with a carefree noise
Dazzled by nothing except
the magic of your spectrum
And the moon with all its pearls fails to
distract me from thinking about you
Oh neighbourhood doe, my charming babe
Are you still remembering the time of friendliness,
When I was kissing roses
in our fragrant love's garden
Sleeping and waking up full of magic ecstasy,
Longing to see your smiling eyes and bright face
Feeling not the life's splendour,
seeing your eyes closed

Until I became a victim of
abandonment and desertion
And saw the sun diving in the horizon saying:
Good-bye, the secrecy and confidentiality of love,
Good-bye until we meet again!!
Note:
Neighbour is an alternative spelling of neighbor. Where neighbor is the preferred spelling in American English, neighbour is the standard in British English.

IN MY EXILE

In my exile,

I got addicted to killing time
So that I might forget the nostalgia to the past
I realized that time does not heal me from depression
Longing, sorrow and sadness
In my exile,
I sat as a hostage in the handcuffs of the past
The clock used to moan with complain
And whine with pain and suffering
In my exile,
Speech faded on my lips
I became an outsider in a strange world
Getting older and older
Time began to stab me more and more
To tie my soul
To tear me more and more
And to hang me on the hooks
In my exile,
My heart was jailed in seventy prisons
Prisons' history did not show similar to them
Curbed my freedom and forced
me to run with the joggers
Prisons' history did not show a prisoner like me
I was imprisoned there
And there were no prisoners except me

In my exile,
I searched for those who imprisoned me
I did not find any of them
Although their voices were like
thunder in my ears for years
I did not see them
Neither in the light of day
Nor in the darkness of the night
They were always sarcastically roaming around me
Sounding profoundly in my ears like an echoing voice
The bells ringing
And the needles pricking
Were they my faithful guardians or my archenemies who had been
imposed on me?
No matter what they were and
what unfairly they could do
I stayed the phoenix of myself,
which is not like the other Phoenicians
I am still and will remain so!!

PHILOSOPHY OF DECEPTION

I am here, my feet are confused
in the momentum of conflict
I lament the insight and look for
the way to escape from being lost
The insight is encircled by pits filled
with the philosophy of deception
The vehicle of truth sinks, without a sail, into the sand
I am here, between my papers and my sick inkwell
My shades dry up over the remains of the old hooks
I doubt even in the remnants of
people and sound ideals
My silence baffles among the
echoes of the deep niches
Pain clashes in my soul and storms in my blood
Ghosts' boilers boil in the corners of my funeral
The luster of the hypocrisy's bracelet
confuses the falsity of the scissor
So I return to devour dirt and abbreviate my silence
I am here, vainly trying to embrace my stars
Believing not in people who
are eaten by echoes of vanity
Believing not in virtues lying
among the folds of the scales

So, I do not ask norms about
the noble ideals and values
Norms are dead and in people's
blood springs of vices flow
They died after missing their
paths and losing all hopes
The laws of modesty dried up and
shined like propaganda
Dull yesterday ceased to exist without a sign!

THE JASMINE'S MANIFESTATIONS

O JASMINE, DON'T EVER CRY

When the jasmine cries
Tears shed fluently now and then
Pain and impatience spread here and there
The place spits us out far away
When the jasmine cries
The hearts break, the minds fly and the bodies shiver
The feelings, desires and passions go back to the past
Security and safety desert us forever
When the jasmine cries
We miss the whisper, smile and tenderness
Joy leaves and the sorrow spreads all around
And we dream of the future
e without hope and contentment
O Damascene and Tunisian jasmine, don't cry
Don't be sad or upset
Don't become depressed or exhausted
,Because of the calamities of aeon
,The recklessness of bats and crows
And bunch of Arabists and traitors
Restore to life its taste and elegance

So, with you, the voices of the pulpits rise
The bells ring in the churches
And the calls to prayers raise in the mosques
How much I adore you jasmine
How much I adore you
With you jasmine, the nightingales sing
The hoopoes hoop
The pigeons coo
And the sparrows tweet
With love, pleasure, longing and patience
The birds spread and chirp in the pastures
In the fields, orchards and gardens
On the bushes and branches of the trees
On the roofs of the castles and palaces
On the balconies of houses and cottages
With you jasmine the tongues
go out from the quarries
The throats shout aloud with thanks and love of God
People become more beautiful, hopeful and faithful
Blessed with the worship of God and
the love of the prophets
Blessed by the recitation and
the intonation of the holy books
So, don't cry
O jasmine, don't ever cry
!!No, no, no, don't cry, now and forever

AHMAD, THE ARABIAN

"Ahmad, The Arabian" is a fictional person wandering among Arab countries to give his opinion on each and evaluate it separately"
O Ahmad, The Arabian,
You are the conscience of homeland
The honour of nations
You are the altruism and chivalry
The Courage and initiation
You are a thousand towering mountains
And a thousand feet and summits
You are the moon
A shining light
A thousand glittering stars
A thousand olive trees
A thousand fig trees
A thousand grape trees
You are a thousand smiles
A warm whisper
A magic musical tune
And a distinguished lovely tone
O Ahmad, The Arabian,
You are a thousand million martyrs
Earth filled the championship
Generations learned how morals are

MAHMOUD S KAWASH

Patriotism and manhood
You are the title of glory
The symbol of civilisation
The role model of humanity
And the example for the new generation
Ahmad, The Arabian,
In Jerusalem, you are a bond and a mobilisation
Buzzing and roaring
Relentless pursuit for struggle
And freedom
In Cairo, you are patience and treachery hurt
Wisdom and farsightedness
Eyesight and insight
Scarf and necklace
In Damascus, you are boom and blast
Waterfall of heroism and energy
Glory and pride
And the call of a mighty giant
In Baghdad, you are a hurricane against evil
Thunder and lightning
Flames of anger
Fire and Light
In Beirut, you are a beacon of culture
Science and art house
Love, optimism and hope
Development and civilisation
In Sana'a, you are a bleeding wound
Pain, patience and hope
A burning ember
And a thousand of sparks
In Tunisia, you are an active ax
A pickaxe

A field for harvest
And sickle
In Algeria, you are the title
of concord and reconciliation
Manhood and ideality
Pride and fairness
Leadership and good omen
In Amman, you are the address of magnanimity
Fragrant perfume
A gushing river
And pure water
In Kuwait, You are the mediator of reconciliation
Among the brothers and neighbours
The title of justice and equality
Luxury, comfort and prosperity
Security and stability
In other Arab countries, you are disappointment
Shame and dullness
Surrender, submissiveness and kneeling
Lack of respect and dignity
Lack of sovereignty and independence.
*Note: "Civilisation, Mobilisation and Neighbourhood" or "Civiliza-
tion, Mobilization and Neighborhood", the first three words are
English and the second three words are American*

IMMORTAL FOREVER

When they asked her about him, she said:
He is immortalised forever
And all others are from a demise
To another demise
He is not a crossbill bird
Rather, the prince of poets to say poetry
Unmatched
No example
The pearl of love on earth
The origin of taste
And perfection
He is the source of inspiration
Revelation
Peace of mind
Rhyme and creativity
Overflow of wisdom
And action
He is a raging fire and flame
The ebb and flow
I'm an ash
A calm blue sea
But in love there is probability
No impossibility
He is a spectrum

A flash of lightning looms in the horizon
Enlightens the gloomy world around
Breaks the restrictions and shackles
Shows glittering bundles of dreams
Gives hope to the future generations
Imagining how he is, I hear an insisting call
Co
ming from the core of my heart
Asking me to change my mind
To come back to my senses
And stop thinking of immigration
Oh God, how do I love him?
How do I while I never met him face to face?
And he is miles and miles away from me
Oh God, what a "promise" the best of words are said about
The most wonderful proverbs are told about too
The space and time are perfumed by its fragrance
It adorns and analyses the people and things
And more and more!!
I yearn to him whenever he calls me
I fell into dreams
I affirm the soul with hopes
Yes, Yes
He is the pearl of love and poetry on earth
He is the origin of taste and perfection too
Yes, Yes
He is as famous as some other contemporary poets
But he is immortal while the others are due to disappear

☆

HOW CAN I FORGET

How can I forget that quiet and romantic night
When my passion called me to the paradise
Of whose spectrum was mixed with my blood
I stood at her door and whispered
Come to the bosom where no one dares to blame
Showing no rejection or hesitation
She hurriedly collapsed and gave herself up
And threw herself in my arms
I sipped the nectar from her lips
So the spittle burst out of the mouth like honey
And she didn't express anger or indignation
Stealing all warmth from her breast
And feeling as if my mouth was burned
I gathered all my courage to embrace her
She swayed brightly and showed all shyness
Then her cheeks seemed as red as the twilight sunset
And its remainder melted in the horizon of the sky
Helen, listen to my whisper in your ears
The flame of love penetrates my heart with pain
I finished my days and your promise is still silent
Hold on my guitar so that it doesn't crash
Helen, be patient and passionate
Hey, enough, you tormented me too much
Join me gently and generously to save my feelings

Haven't I woven my feelings a ladder for you to climb
Didn't I keep going and coming waiting your promised longing
I kissed her until I became drunken by her breathes
My limbs loosened and my thirst quenched
So, how can I forget that quiet night!!
Surely I can't!!

MY CHEEKY REBEL
SHADOW

My shadow rebelled with yielding shadows
Oh my heart, while my secret might be broadcast
It would be tired of being estranged with me
Unless it walked the paths with conviction
I moved my head, it didn't move its head
I jumped, it didn't jump, it revolted and didn't obey
I ran far away, it stayed constant in its place
I walked a long distance, it didn't walk an inch
I tried with my shadow for a long time
I blamed it, showed it too much kindness
But it kept refusing to accompany me
It showed deafness and refused to listen
Everyone was accompanied by his shadow except me
I was suffering from the desertion of my shadow
Everyone was pushing his shadow forward
Encouraging it and bringing it to the arena of conflict
Except me, I was left without shadow and mask
I tried to pull it out of the cruelty of desertion
I tried to call it as the beau calls his sweetheart
I tried to plead with it as the sailor invokes the sail
I vainly tried, but my cheeky shadow
sold me in an instant
Oh Lord, I didn't know how it sold me!!

MAHMOUD S KAWASH

LONGING STRIKES
MY CHEST

"!!A dialogue between two lovers"

:He said to her
O sweetheart, O magic chant
Who dissolves and scatters in the cup of my youth
?Aren't you caring for my love, O fragrant rose
Your breathtaking beauty seem bewitching
Longing strikes my chest while you are afar
And the emotion whispers throughout my eyelids
!?Is there anything to say after this estrangement of both hearts
O heart, be quiet and put the pain and blame aside
O heart, the beloved is leading her soldiers to the battlefield of ha-
tred
!?Do I miscalculate and misunderstand the situation
Is it a real estrangement, or seems so because you are a different
?woman
Good morning and evening
my happiness and contentment
:She replied
Good morning and
evening of longing, emotion and affection
No, no, good morning and evening of real love and life

!!You talk about estrangement
?How do you suggest that
,How do you delude this estrangement
!!oh you all love
!!I love you, only you and no other
?I love you!! Do you understand
?I'm a different woman!! Do you understand
A woman who loves you and can't live without you
A woman who loves your world
Who can't be far away from you
!!Excuse me, I'm a different woman
Yes, I'm a different woman who
follows your footsteps
!!And do more and more
I'm a woman who has no life without you
A woman who spends the nights dreaming of you
A woman who hopes to keep warm beside you
Doesn't stop thinking about you
so as not to forget you
!!Excuse me, I'm a different woman
A woman who doesn't speak other
than the language of lovers
Your smile makes me mesmerized
by the most beautiful looks
A woman who aspires to see you day and night
!!Excuse me I'm a different woman
,I'm a woman, different from the women of these days
Fits you as a man different
!!from the men of these days
And because I'm a different
!!woman I love you, different man
?How much do I love you!! Do you understand

!!Surely you understand!! I'm sure you understand

SELF DIALOGUE...THE MOON SHONE

When she appeared with her magical
,look as the sun rises at dawn
The eyes popped, the necks rose up
and the chests flared
When she walked and saddled
like a beautiful peacock
She looked like an elderberry blossom "trimming its branches and
"brushing its leaves
Then, the sceptre bent, the earth stretched out in the arms of the
encounter and the hearts melted
The minds were lost and the
wise men and their wisdom vanished
The lamps of light became faint and
dim in the depth of the soul
The lighthouses, the traffic lights
went out and the candles melted
The tambourines tinkled and the drums beat
The music played Beethoven's symphony
"The Moonlight"
"The walls of the heart danced the "Penguin Dance
The heart's rooms astonishingly and deliriously cried
,The rhymes and poetry collapsed

contracted and cocooned
The strings and the roads intertwined
The doors, windows and all entrances were sealed
The calls to prayer went out of the mosques and the bells rang in
the churches
The cheeks were scented with
the most luxurious perfume
The fingers became wet with the nectar of violets, jasmines and all
sorts of flowers
The eyes clang to the infinities of distances
,The moon glowed at the top of the sky
Above it was a smile of hope and
optimism about the future
Then, as an angel, she twinkled, dangled with her splendid stature
!!and disappeared
Congratulations to her, congratulations to me
.Congratulations to everyone who loved or knew her
Note: "Sceptre" is used in the English literature and "Scepter" is used
.in the American literature

THE VIOLETS' MANIFESTATIONS

Violets!! Oh violets!!
Why violets? Oh why!!?
Oh violets oh!!
Yah, oh violets oh!!
Violets have a long history
Growing and infinitive
They are of beautiful types and colors
Wonderful and do not accept the alternatives
Violets brightly decorate the plains
The valleys and the mountains
They take rest on the hills and the sandy beaches
Fill the gardens and the groves
Some are white, others are yellow
Some are wild, others are tri-color
Some grow in the forests, others grow in the fields
Some are flowers, others are trees
Their fragrance refreshes the hearts and minds
Violets are the melodies of the long palms
The warm whisper of hope
The tickle of the fresh gushing water
Hearts beating with love
Usually optimistic, not pessimistic
And never be depressed

Violets are homing pigeon cooers
The twitters of birds enjoying freedom
The playing of the charming guitars
In all the circumstances, they are near not far
Reassuring peace and stable security
Violets are an auspicious past
Smiling and pure present and a blissful future
An impressionable pride and so high in the sky
Blessed by the angels
By the people all around
And by God before both of them
Violets look like the cute young girls
Crowds of dancers on wonderful dance halls
Generations after generations of companions
Renewal after renewal of a magic Parisian perfume
Compassionate and loving hearts and celibate lovers
Violets have their own styles, signs and rituals
They are the cause and the solution
The source of inspiration
The disease and recovery
The medicine, treatment and care
Violets are the truth and reality
Neither a heresy nor a lie
They are miracles
Upside down standards
Seeking and obeying violets,
everything with you turns well
Violets are the dew and flamboyance
Sweetness and kindness
Delicacy and glamour
Permanent presence
Brilliance and handsomeness

Glowing and cresting
Spinning the robe of love
Violets are Fire, light and water
Dust and air
Flood of spirits that transcend the sky
The chain and the title of glory and dignity
The judgment of the place and time
The illuminated dreams
Violets are abounding longings
Perfumed scattered whispers
Noble, courageous and brazen
Generous to the extent of altruism
Bold, brave and mighty knights
They attack bravely and do not flee
Violets have glowing radiance and luminous energy
Never being harmed by simplicity or ignorance
Need no more awareness or
nobility to shine and glitter
Their lights depend on their gorgeous gestures
With them you get justice, safety and integrity
Courage, affliction and power
They are bouquets which snuff out in the vases
Violets!! Oh violets!!
Why violets? Oh why!!
Oh violets oh!!
Yah, oh violets oh!!

THE VIOLETS' LOVER

Oh violets' lover, come hurriedly and dwell inside me
All that in the heart annoys and causes pain to me
Oh the tattoo of the soul that
tortures and exhausts me
?Isn't it more than enough for you and me
Oh life, don't you realise that I'm holding on to you
!!Through my sanity, madness and nostalgia
Don't you see that I'm sailing as a boat in a rough sea
Lost in futility of sorrows, searching for you
To become happy, enjoying the flames of love
Which burns me and enriches me with its warmth
Oh love, oh, oh and oh
!!Is it love or a special form of madness
Oh violets' lover, listen well to understand me
And to take me to a place of peace and tranquility
I got bored of everything in this universe, except you
,O king of feelings, o pure of heart
o tenderhearted one
Please come as quickly as you can
Come to accompany me to the altar of love
Where we pray and reveal our hidden emotions
Oh violets' lover, to whom I vowed all my lifetime
Your prison is different from all prisons
.Yes, it is surely different from all other prisons

All the roses and blossoms are gifts for you
The blue sea and green land are at your command
The ebbs and tides calm down for a look of your eyes
Everything in the universe is at your order
!!All are to you with all love, you the violets' lover

A COINCIDENCE OR A SHOT WITHOUT A SHOOTER?

That day I did what I did not plan to do
With all my madness, stubbornness and rebellion
I scattered my fragrance and
the breeze of my affection
That day I preferred something that you showed me
Purposely and previously planned or accidently
But it was tasteful, useful and good to me
With all patience and flirtation of a loving heart
I drew orchards and fields of grandeur and sadness
Then with longing groans I recited the verses of love
And chanted hymns of happiness, hope and optimism
Then I threw myself towards you
That day my heart was flying seeking meadows
Looking for a fragrance in which hope would revive
Every whisper of mine sought to the
verses of magic and adoration
And everything remained fine
until the surprise happened
When my boat crashed on the
rubble of a painful song
And my heart became wounded,
disappointed and desperate

Oh my fools, oh!!
How did I wake up from my dream while I was not yet eighteen
How? How?
How could I mature again after that day, how?
How? How?
How could I dream of a ship, a sail and an anchor
When all my scents have been burned
And their aromas dried out
among the incense burners?
The painful talking was silently
cutting the links of the heart
As I stared at the features of your face and listened to your warm,
even burning whispers!!
Was it a coincidence or a shot without a shooter?
Or you see it as a fabrication of a day
in which no one is to be blamed?!
God knows, the one who alone knows
Glory be to God in the highest and peace on earth

THE DAIALOGUE
HAS A REST

When I asked her about herself and her heart's news she said:
In the past, I used to listen to the stories of lovers
To write down their conversations and transform them into love
stories
To spin roses with which I would decorate my hair
And to color my diaries with
But I forgot that I was a part of those stories
Which they lived and told, while
I was the heroine therein
Even more, their main components were some passions which
shook me
Embraced my feelings and spied on my soul
Although I hoped that one day
I would share the lovers' traits
I vainly tried to achieve them and
there was no hope or benefit
The past was over and turned into memories
The present shows no optimism and
no great expectations
The future will be murky and without clear features
While you and I are no more than two symbols
Who occupy two pawns in a game of chess
In which we may become prisoners

Or perhaps one will gain the status of the king and ascend the
throne
The other will attain the rank of the ordinary pawn
No doubt that both matters can only be achieved
With a hymn in a word game and a table of pawns!!
The glory is to God, in the heaven and on the earth
The dialogue is not finished yet and
the rest may come later!!

NOTHING REMAINS
EXCEPT YOUR
CHARM

O you, who possesses both, the heart and the tongue!!
In your presence the sun and
the moon lose their luster
They bow down of respect for you
They flee away ashamed of your beauty
The stars and planets keep silent
out of respect for you too
The mixtures and components physically mix together
The compounds chemically react and
dissolve forming new ones
In your presence the solids melt and turn into liquids
The liquids evaporate and turn into gases
The gases spread all around in the atmosphere
Even the equations overlap and
get lost with each other
The chains and barriers break and fall down
The dams and borders collapse
In your presence the logic
loses its value and disappears
The forms of linguistic and
intellectual pluralism freeze
The culture loses its potency and influence

The words and their meanings lose their vitality
The circles of knowledge,
encyclopedias and dictionaries cease
Nothing remains as it is except your charm
Which rises up and soars above the clouds !!

MY INCENSE
BURNERS WERE
BURNT OUT

When they met after a long absence he said to her:
I was living in the flame of suspicion and anxiety
Drunken wandering alone in void valleys
My incense burners were burnt and
their scent was dried out
The distance between the incense burners and the communication
was afar
My boats waddled through the futility of melancholy
Lazy and wretched, sailed homelessly in the fog
Playing the loyalty melody,
I returned with trembling fingertips
The melody of remembrance passed through the night of my ob-
sessions
And was awakened by the promised love and passion
Then he added:
O you fragrance of longing,
have a nice morning and evening
O you honey and antidote of life,
have a wonderful morning and evening
Morning and evening of different flowers and the soul with differ-
ent feelings and sensations
Morning and evening of longing and thirst of love

With all that you show of calmness and madness
Morning and evening of love my sweetheart
She replied him saying:
Your morning and evening are as you are, pure, innocent and cour-
teous
You make me live among your
magic letters and words
You make me listen to them,
breathe them and melt in them
O you the limit of love
How wonderful your expressions are!!
How wonderful your feelings are!!
They dance on the walls of my heart and
all others' hearts
How wonderful you are when you write and become full of deli-
cious flavor, as I imagine
O you creative, your mornings
and evenings are charming
Your nights are warm, romantic,
amusing and more and more
God bless you and many thanks to you
I greet you and I am grateful for
your pure and white heart
I love you, how much do I love you!!
I miss you, how much do I miss you!!
O God, how beautiful you are and
how torment is your soul
How sweet your mornings and evenings are
How sweet they are!!
How sweet!! How sweet!!

O THE LIMIT OF LOVE, MY ONLY LOVE

He said to her:

O you exceptional woman, with your beauty and charm
Your morning is hope, happiness and contentment
Your morning is an orchard of roses,
flowers and fragrances
All your times, are purple bouquets
I love and Jasmine's bunches I adore!!
O you exceptional woman,
with your morals and characters
Your last message burst my heart
with longing and nostalgia for you
Since then, your spectrum
did not leave my imagination
Used to caress my dreams and
dance on the passions of my heart
O you exceptional woman,
the descendant of roses and rubies
Do not ever prolong your absence
or decrease your love to me
Listen to my warm whispers tickling your feelings
Listen to my heart beating with love to you
O you exceptional woman,
whose nostalgia is all around
Awaiting you in the agony of a longing lover
I made my feelings a ladder for you to ascend

My fragrant whispers carried all the warmth to you
To extinguish the thirst of your hungry heart
I am missing you honey...
I am missing you more and more!!
So many kisses to you and as them flowers to you too
Do you think this has some impact on your heart?
She replied him saying:
O the limit of love, all love and my only love
Your words are still having
the impact and the influence
More than you and I may think or expect
May God bless you and all your steps in life
Many thanks for your good taste
and your sublime kindness
Thanks in the size of all the epics in all languages
They control our presence here, there and everywhere
To remain together and no one dares to disturb us
So please stop pushing me and take it easy with me
Then I can be able to keep up with you
To respond to you and your satisfaction too
God bless you, me and our exceptional love!!

THE FRIENDS ARE EITHER BLESSINGS OR CURSES

"Life is a circle of giving and taking!!"

Our hearts do not hurt, it is our brains which do
Let us be positive and make
people happy with our humanity
Let us accustom ourselves to smile and be cheerful
There is no charge for a little laugh or a simple smile
One or both can change the life
of someone here or there
Do your best to distance yourself from negativity
That is the only way to
achieve inner peace and tranquility
The friends are either blessings or curses
Some come as heavy burdens and abuse our life
Others come as gifts and give us useful lessons
The second kind makes us aware,
keeping our eyes opened
It makes us realise that people are not the same
That life is different according to times and places
That there are complications
in our way to achieve success
As long as we believe in God, our only saviour
We keep smiling to our successes as well as to our fails
We keep doing our best to help staying real humans
I wish I could soar as high in the sky as I possibly can

Where there is no harm or disturbance, with birds
Where I can touch the stars, day and night
Where I sit with angels and bring peace in every heart
As long as we believe in God, our only saviour
We need to learn to let bad things burn
We need to thank people who cause harm to us
They make us better,
stronger and never trust them again
We need to forgive them and
let them go free, live and grow
Thanks to them, because
we owe them that we get better
It should be so, because life is a circle of giving and taking!!

KEEP LOVING, SMILING AND HELPING

"Power is not in muscles, wealth or position"
In life, I meet ups and downs
I see good and bad days
I don't get everything I want
But I get what I need
I wake up with some aches and pains
But I wake up
My life may not be perfect
But I am blessed and happy
There are countless planets and stars in the universe
Each has its own place, importance and it is unique
Every single person has a special place
and role in the world
No matter who is he, he is equally important as others
We are all "a planet or a shining star"
in someone's life
Be positive and never hesitate
to help those who need you
So, God may bless you and make you happy
I don't really understand how

someone can tell so many lies
Without blinking, hesitating and being shameful
Or regretful and feel bad about that
Power is not in muscles, wealth or position
So show your personality through
giving and helping others
Be a handful of goodness and blessings
To relieve the burdens you carry
on your shoulders and be blessed
Neither the nights nor the
problems can defeat sunrise or hope
So try and never lose hope to
achieve what you dream of
Even if you don't achieve it,
at least you try your best
And will not regret to leave this world
Life is too short like a Sunrise to Sunset
Keep loving, Smiling, helping and
stay away from negativity
May God bless you and make you happy

A DIFFERENT WOMAN

After tracing her and following
her steps for a long time
I approached her courtly and
initiated contact, saying:
"Hey you angelic princess
I'm hopefully looking for the sister of the moon
My eyes have not seen such a beautiful face
Do I find acceptance in your life, my angel?"
She realised my intention and hurried along
So, she began to step in front of me in fury and pride
Then she turned towards a dark path
Where the voice was scarce, as people were few
I continued to follow her steps
She slowed down and turned back,
expressing caution!!
Then she paused and said nervously,
firmly and strictly:
"Excuse me, I'm a different woman
Who does not love or dream of you
Who does not want to see or meet you
I'm a serious woman who does not think of you!!
Excuse me, I'm a different woman
Who is not fluent in the language of love

Different from the women of these days
I'm a woman who knows many things
Other than dreams and fantasies!!
Excuse me, I'm another woman
Who does not speak the language of lovers
Who is not a prey to be easily hunted
Or to fall in your nets or traps, you foul
The road to me is paved with thorns, not roses!!
Excuse me I'm a different woman
Who is neither interested in your smile
Nor charmed by your beautiful looks
Who is steadfast in her faith as the moored mountain
And never responds to the temptations you offer!!
Really, I'm a different woman
Who knows her Creator well and never disobey
Who doesn't commit sins or fall in troubles
I'm a woman who doesn't dream of love
Except when I'm brought closer to heaven
So I may be crammed with good fortified women!!

SHE IS A WOMAN...WHAT A WOMAN!!

She loves him so, because she understands love so
She instinctively, innocently and purely loves him
She dreamily, delicately,
freshly and honestly loves him
She loves him with all her pride, glory and humility
She loves him when she is strong, weak and sick
She loves him the way she likes and used to
She loves him with a warm romance, tenderness and chastity
What a woman she is!! She's really a woman.
She loves him so, because she's such a woman
She's half real sane and half fictional
She's half wise and half simple minded Bedouin
She's half outrageous and half quiet civilised
She's half a tied prisoner and half a modern princess
She's half a naive child and half a genius woman
Shortly she sincerely and spontaneously loves him
What a woman she is!! She's really a woman.
She loves him so, because she is so
What a wonderful woman she is
She's wonderful with her negatives
She's wonderful and pretty cool with her positives
She's wonderful with her virtues and sins

Isn't she a wonderful woman? She really is!!
What a woman she is!! She's really a woman
May God, the saviour bless her and him.

WHICH READS FIRST, THE HEART OR THE SIGHT?

With you, life is blessed and has the fragrance of faith
Crammed with confusion, bewilderment and anxiety
You are the pearl of oceans and
the secret of beauty on earth
How splendid the poem becomes
when your letters adorn it
When it turns into a bow that hits
with the arrows of rhymes
When it becomes a bullet that goes without a deadline
When life begins with it and
knows no end or limit of time
How powerful your pen becomes when its ink flows
Draws you magical pulses inside me
Writes you golden verses on the strings of my heart
Makes roses grow on my cheeks
Makes almonds bloom on my mouth
Makes the drip drips from between my lips
Makes questions overrun over the fringes of my eyes
Glows and spreads light of optimism in my soul
Slides a burning flame on the snow of my heart
Then excites it and sets fire inside its four rooms!!
Oh the angelic prince of my heart
Am I not the neighbourhood doe who loves you
Who searches refuge from
thirst in your pastoral fields
Am I not wandering among
the sides of your meadows

Looking for water, because
you are the rain and the blessing
Aren't your letters looking like
diamonds in form and content
While I am monotheistic in your own world
Life is now reduced to a gesture from you
When it was not reduced before
to a gesture from the moon
Not even from the deafening
stone or the echo in a deep valley
O silent sea, I know that your
waves indicate the start, not the end
You should know that the
heart is no longer asking the eyes:
Is it ebb or tide and which reads your letters first,
the heart or the sight?
Note: This poem was published in (Whisper of Soflay – volume 4 – yearly anthology – 2022 – pages 362, 363 and 364)

MY NOSTALGIA FOR YOU!!

When your absence complies with
me in the presence of longing
The letters of my poem wear your perfume
The strings of pens head on lines towards you
To form a letter that leans on my soft spring shadow
Which searches for you behind the desert silence
To let me live in an oasis of leaves
I water with a blossom that
bears the flavor of my blood
My nostalgia for you is a letter which
pours out the river of my flowers
Draws the first smile that sees the sunrise of life
As if you are the first word to
inhabit the dictionary of love
The moment in which my eyes fall asleep
The vision which reflects itself on the edge of my pen
The ink pot that utters the
meanings carrying your flavour
Most probably the spirit was indwelling you until it touched you to
give birth
Yes, I will break silence as long as you are with me
To practice the ritual of splashing ink with you

To stimulate poetically the
pulse of moments inside you
And no matter how the footsteps of that pen go,
I will travel with you
To share my covenant with you
To keep pouring my soul with you
To draw you letters in the colour of the sky
Oh man, whom I failed to place in my chest,
so my poetry recited him
My message to you is sinking between
a dream and a sea of papers!!

Note: This poem was published in (Atuns Galaxy Anthology – 2022 – Anthology of contemporary world poetry – Atuns poetry - pages 228 and 229)